T0193597

What Does

Have to Do with It?

Understanding and Operating in the Power of God

VERNADETTE AUGUSTUSEL

WESTBOW
PRESS®
A DIVISION OF THOMAS NELSON
& ZONDERVAN

WestBow Press books may be ordered through booksellers or by contacting:

WestBow Press
A Division of Thomas Nelson & Zondervan
1663 Liberty Drive
Bloomington, IN 47403
www.westbowpress.com
844-714-3454

Scripture quotations taken from The Holy Bible, New International
Version® NIV® Copyright © 1973 1978 1984 2011 by Biblica,
Inc. TM. Used by permission. All rights reserved worldwide.

Scripture taken from the New King James Version® Copyright ©
1982 by Thomas Nelson. Used by permission. All rights reserved.

Scripture taken from the Amplified Bible, Copyright © 1954, 1958, 1962,
1964, 1965, 1987 by The Lockman Foundation. Used with permission.

ISBN: 978-1-6642-3075-0 (sc)
ISBN: 978-1-6642-3074-3 (e)

Library of Congress Control Number: 2021907563

Print information available on the last page.

WestBow Press rev. date: 04/23/2021

Contents

In a twenty-year life span of being saved for real, God has helped me to understand and realize that our love walk is vital and very important to our spiritual development and growth. Through various relationships, I've come to understand that we, as Christians, are not walking in love the way God has intended. Too often, many of us claim to be saved and have a serious relationship with God, yet we walk in hatred, jealousy, and strife at the same time. Far too many brothers and sisters in the body of Christ are rejoicing over the failure, fall, and weakness of each other. It grieves the very heart of God to see his children not walking in sincere love toward each other, ourselves, and, ultimately, God our Father. Now is the time to live and operate in the kingdom of God, here on earth, since we are the sons and daughters of God. When we compete with each other instead of complementing each other, we are not operating in kingdom business. Rather, we have seriously missed God and have now crossed over into operating in the kingdom of darkness without ever realizing it.

One day, the love-walk message began to come to me as I was preparing to leave for the West Coast with my oldest son. He had just finished high school, and he had hopes of going away to a nice school for the arts in California. It had never occurred to me, however, that some people around me did not expect very much from my life or my children's lives until we landed an interview with a very nice school. Some people began to act indifferent toward us because we were preparing to leave for the West Coast. During that time, we were struggling. We struggled just to get our son through high school. Then we struggled with having enough money for our round-trip tickets, the car rental, and hotel. Bottom line: at one time, we struggled financially. It all was a big struggle for us, but God somehow worked it all out. So why would anyone be jealous of us instead of praying for us? This was what I could not understand.

As word got out that we were going to California for a mini-vacation and interview with a potential school, I guess you would say some people were jealous and hateful. They really were not happy or celebratory for us. Since then, I've taken note that some people react at good things and when things are going well for you. Jealousy came from people who had a lot more going for them than we did. At that time, people were experiencing blessings or being blessed in the very ways we only imagined or hoped to be.

Nevertheless, to my surprise, some were not so happy to see God bless my family and me. I could not understand—or perhaps I was being naive, not realizing that some Christian people can operate in ill feelings and not operate in the spirit of love. As Christians, we expected jealousy to come from the world but not from our brothers and sisters in Christ. My heart aches when I see those of us who supposedly stand for God in love act so petty toward others. God desires to see his children operating in love, demonstrating his power and authority in the earthly realm.

We had a wonderful time while we were away, but the love message God birth in me would not leave me alone. The love message, from biblical times till now, will always be relevant and never get old or go away. The spirit of love will heal you and set you free, if only you allow it to minister to you. As I reflected on what God had birthed in me—the message of love—I prayed, read, and meditated on the love of God. God will use situations, circumstances, and daily life experiences to teach you about the healing power of his divine love. Will you allow and trust in the healing power of God's love for your life?

We were created with two natures; but we are three part beings. We are a spirit first, and our spirit man lives in a body, our natural man; our natural man possesses a soul. The old man, our old nature, the natural man, cannot operate out of a spirit of true love, nor can it coexist or cohabitate with the new man, regenerated man, or the spiritual man, who has been renewed in the Spirit and changed, born again in the Spirit of the living God. The spirit man operates in the Spirit of Christ Jesus because he has been renewed in the spirit of his mind.

> And be continually renewed in the spirit of your mind [having a fresh, untarnished mental and spiritual attitude]. (Ephesians 4:23 AMP)

> The old man will not operate in a spirit of love, no matter what. The old man, our old nature, can put up with appearances but for so long of a loving person, no matter how easy it may be. The new man, however, our new nature, can and will operate in a spirit of love, no matter what or how hard it may become because the new man will operate in love with the supernatural help of God. The new man will not attempt to do anything without the help of God or the absence of his presence. That's why he can operate in the supernatural love.

One

The Power of Love

Psalm 139:14
1 Corinthians 13:4–8
Mark 12:28–33
Mathew 22:37
Romans 13:8–10
1 Corinthians 13:8
Galatians 5:13–14
3 John 1:2

God is calling us to a radical love walk. What is love? Well, according to the Word of God, love is several different things. In 1 Corinthians 13:4–8 (AMP), I believe we have a good picture of true love:

> Love endures with patience and serenity, love is kind and thoughtful, and is not jealous or envious; love does not brag and is not proud or arrogant. It is not rude; it is not self-seeking, it is not provoked [nor

overly sensitive and easily angered]; it does not take into account a wrong endured. It does not rejoice at injustice, but rejoices with the truth [when right and truth prevail]. Love bears all things [regardless of what comes], believes all things [looking for the best in each one], hopes all things [remaining steadfast during difficult times], endures all things [without weakening], Love never fails.

Now that we have an idea of what love is, look at what love is not. It is not manipulation, deceit, hatred, jealous, envy, strife, rebellion, discord, control, greed, betrayal, or selfishness. Love is a spirit, and the Bible says that God is love.

The one who does not love has not become acquainted with God [does not and never did know Him], for God is love. [He is the originator of love, and it is an enduring attribute of His nature.] (1 John 4:8 AMP)

So that would make love alive and active, a spiritual force. And where there is love, there is the presence and power of almighty God.

As we allow the power of God's love to flow through our lives, we can experience joy and excitement for living. Like the old song says, "This joy that I have, the world did not give it to me and the world cannot take it away." This is so true because the realization of God's love will give you joy for living, no matter what situation or circumstance you may be facing. The love of God will always bring victorious living. When you become aware of God's love, it will bring a sense of peace—an unexplainable sense of peace. Many people too often don't have a zeal for living. Some just go through life by existing from one day to the next, simply because they do not realize how much God loves them and how much he wants his love to flow in and through their lives.

God's love is one of the first spiritual gifts to humanity, but most of us don't acknowledge the depth of God's love, simply because we don't realize that it is a spiritual force with power and anointing abilities. And because we have not acknowledged God's love, we cannot operate in the power and authority that he has given us on earth. What we need to do is give up our hang-ups, get together, and serve God and each other in the spiritual force of love. If we could just understand that when we are scheming, plotting, backbiting, and harboring jealousy and hatred toward each other, the kingdom of darkness is advancing. But if we learn to walk in God's love, the kingdom of heaven advances. One quick question: whose side are you working on? Let's get together on kingdom business and work on the Lord's side to bring the kingdom of God here on earth.

When we are not walking in God's love, his spiritual force, we are actually working against God, the Father, and his kingdom. Either we are for God, by walking in his divine love, Holy Spirit, and force, or we are working for Satan, harboring ill feelings and operating in evilness. Quick question again: whose side are you working on?

The fruit of the Spirit is love. A good example of walking in God's love is in Galatians 5:22–23. We are reminded of what the fruit of the Spirit, love, produces if we walk in it. But the fruit of the Spirit is love, and love will produce other godly attributes like joy, peace, patience, kindness, goodness, faithfulness, gentleness, and self-control.

> But the fruit of the Spirit [the result of His presence within us] is love [unselfish concern for others], joy, [inner] peace, patience [not the ability to wait, but how we act while waiting], kindness, goodness, faithfulness, gentleness, self-control. Against such things there is no law. (Galatians 5:22–23 AMP)

Everything God the Father wanted to teach us is based wholly on love: our love for him, our love for others, and our love for ourselves. We should know we are beautifully and wonderfully made by God himself (Psalm 139:14). In Hebrews 10:24, the Word says, "And let us consider [thoughtfully] how we may encourage one another to love and to do good deeds."

The Word of God also reminds us that the greatest commandment to keep is to walk in love (Mark 12:28–33; Matthew 22:37; Romans 13:8–10; Galatians 5:13–14). Without love, we have nothing because anything absent from love is without God. The very existence of God is exemplified in love. Everything in the kingdom is based on love, and we have nothing without love, not even access to kingdom benefits and certain blessings.

In Mark 12:34, when Jesus was being questioned about which of the commandments was the greatest, he told the religious teachers that the greatest of all commandments is to walk in love. And believe it or not, that's just where your healing is: your blessings, your peace, and your prosperity as your soul prospers. In 3 John 1:2 (AMP), as God's beloved children, John writes, "Beloved, I pray that in every way you may succeed and prosper and be in good health [physically], just as [I know] your soul prospers [spiritually]." Now, how can we say that we are for God and not walk in the fruit of the Spirit, the power of God's love? How can we say we know God and not practice his presences by walking in love? Because when we practice walking in love, we exercise the fruit of the Spirit; we are actually practicing being in God's presence.

The entire Word of God is summed up in a single command: "For the entire law is fulfilled in keeping this one command: 'Love your neighbor as yourself'" (Galatians 5:14).

Friend, examine your love walk. If someone is walking in hatred, envy, cheating, and greed, just to name a few, their love walk is out of order. Get back in line with God, and start practicing his presence by walking in his love. So many people miss out on the greatest love affair of a lifetime because they don't acknowledge God's love. We must examine ourselves and allow the love of God to flow in and through our lives.

Oh, by the way, God plays for keeps. He is not looking for any part-time loves. So if you think of skipping out on God, and two-timing him, it's best that you don't mess with him in any kind of way. We need to be consumed with the love of God or leave it alone. Just as Jesus was a living example of God's love, we are to be examples also.

Our love walk is very important to our Christian walk

and spiritual growth. The more of God's love we walk in, the more we grow spiritually. As we walk in God's love, the evidence of his presence and power is made manifest in and through our lives. If we will allow God, his love will transform us. As more of the transformation takes place, we become more like him. God intends for us to be transformed into his image more and more. I believe that causes us to repent. God's goodness demonstrates his love shown toward us. This love, once experienced, will cause one to become a new person in Christ Jesus. As we allow God's love to transform us, his power will flow in and through our lives to change things for the better.

Love will always affect our quality of life, including how well and how long we live. Some people have literally died from broken hearts, as they felt as though no one truly loved them. Perhaps they never experienced how to love God or themselves. Sadly, they did not come to know and understand that God's love was available to them. Love is a very important part of life. As we develop, it is very important that we experience love, but most important, we need to experience God's love. As we read a little farther, we will discover several types of love.

It is my belief that if someone was raised in an atmosphere of love or maybe experiences love later on in life, he or she would normally have a healthy lifestyle. Healthy emotions and a sense of well-being, I believe, are signs of someone experiencing love and care. People who have been abused emotionally, mentally, and/or physically are normally afraid to love because they don't know if they can ever trust themselves to love again. They are afraid of being hurt again.

Trust is a major part of love, and people who have been

hurt don't want to hurt anymore. To keep from being hurt again from the lack of love, these people will put up different defense mechanisms to guide their hearts and feelings. So many people today are afraid to love; they are afraid of true love. Maybe they will try surface love because it does not require sacrifice like true love. Most people are not willing to sacrifice anything these days, not even their feelings being temporarily hurt. They desire and want love more than anything, but they are in a prison from past experience of no love, so they refuse to walk in love or allow themselves to be loved. These people see no way of ever getting out from the prison of no love.

Dear friend, there is a way out, and it is through Jesus Christ. Jesus is the way, the truth, and the light; he came to set the captives free. As the Word says, whomever Jesus set free is free indeed. You may ask yourself how to get out of the prison of no love. Well, just call on the name of the Lord Jesus right where you are. Ask him for help, and be truthful with him. Tell him that you want out of the prison of no love and that you want to love again, like experiencing love for the very first time. Tell him that you need to experience love and give love but that you don't really know how or where to begin.

As we open ourselves up to love, we must understand that pain and hurt may come, but that is a part of life and love. We must realize to be loved and receive or give love as if no one will or has ever hurt us is a leap of faith. When we open ourselves to God's love, the spirit of love will flow in and through our lives. In this process of learning to love, we must learn to overlook people's offenses because if we don't, we will walk around in the bondage and pain of people hurting us. We must grow a stronger backbone in the spiritual realm; learn to just stand up in God's love because his love will never fail us.

Every day, practice overlooking the pain of someone who may be trying to hurt you and cause you pain. This will keep you free from the spirit of offense. In other words, learn to forgive as much as possible. Sometimes in life, in order for us to move on to a higher plane, we just have to overlook people's ignorance and offenses. Believe it or not, some pain that people will try to cause you may be intentional. I'm not saying to allow yourself to be abused by people, but there is a way of maneuvering yourself around abusive people that will not cause you to become bitter and revengeful, unforgiving, and not loving. The Spirit of God always gives us wisdom, if we ask. Without the help of the Holy Spirit, we can do nothing, for he's the third person of the divine Trinity, giving us strength—supernatural strength—to do what needs to be done.

Once you are out of the prison of no love, you must make sound decisions and be determined that you are never going back behind those bars of imprisonment again. Fight the good faith fight to love and be loved; fight for your freedom to experience the anointing of God's love flowing through you because the fight to love is a daily battle. Every day of your life, you will be faced with the choice of holding on to pain and hurt from the past or present to walk in love. Sometimes, others will bring you their pain and hurt, just to see what you will do with it, or they may want to cause you the pain they are feeling. Hurting people will hurt people. There are some who don't believe in love, only pain, because they are fearful. But reject it and show them the depths of God's love.

The power of God's love can conquer all things, but we must have faith in it. The Bible tells us that it is impossible to please God without faith. Well, faith in what? For one, we must have faith in the power of God's love and have faith that God's love is real and begin to operate in it. If we do not exercise faith in the power of God's love and the fact that it is real, it cannot and will not work for us. Faith without work is dead.

> As the body without the spirit is dead, so
> faith without deeds is dead. (James 2:26)

Each day, we must make a choice to do something with the pain and hurt in our lives. What are you going to do with it? Will you begin each day with hope and a commitment to walk in God's love, or will you go back to the prison of no love? We walk in God's love by communicating with him daily through prayer, reading, and meditating on his Word. Spend some time with him so that he can empower you to walk in his love. This is the only way to stay free to love God's way. To walk in God's love is to walk in the supernatural. If you try to love in your own ability, you will fail to operate in true love. But remember God's love is supernatural and a powerful force. His love is his spirit and his presence that is alive and active, which helps or empowers us to love when love seems impossible.

We can walk in God's love and move by his power in several ways.

Be aware of your inner person, your spiritual person.

Take a daily assessment of where you are spiritually, and be truthful with yourself. If something is not right in your spirit, repent and get yourself together.

Be committed to daily devotions through prayer and reading and studying the Word of God. Communicate daily with God. Meditate on his love for you and his promises. Listen to the Word; speak and confess the Word over yourself.

Submit and surrender any and all ill feelings you may be harboring. Cleanse your heart daily. Psalm 51:10 reminds us to ask God if you are harboring any ill feelings like King David did when he knew things within himself, his heart, was not right.

Create in me a clean heart, O God, and renew a right and steadfast spirit within me. (Psalm 51:10 AMP)

In order for God to pour his love in our hearts, we must allow our hearts to be cleared out, purged of all that illness. God's love cannot come into a place filled with ill feelings and evilness. Make sure your heart is right or that you want to get right.

Walk in forgiveness, and practice being kind to others. Learn to smile and learn to laugh again. Lift up your head and live again; there is always something to live for. Ecclesiastes 9:4 says, "Anyone who is among the living has hope—even a live dog is better off than a dead lion!"

Daily, cast your cares and anxieties on God the Father. First Peter 5:7 says, "Cast all your anxiety on him because he cares for you."

Be prayerful and thankful about everything.

Rejoice always and delight in your faith; be unceasing and persistent in prayer; in every situation [no matter what the circumstances] be thankful and continually give thanks to God; for this is the will of God for you in Christ Jesus. (1 Thessalonians 5:16–18 AMP)

Learn to trust God to help you love the unlovable. Remember to ask God to help you walk in his love. Practice, practice, practice walking in love because practice makes perfect; and / or brings maturity in a thing that you practice. So practice your love walk; it will make you mature in love. Never give up; always keep trying to grow in your love walk.

Remember that love never fails, but we fail to love. Understand that if you give love and sow love, it will find its way back to you. You always reap what you have sown.

Two

Lord, Teach Us How to Love

1 Corinthians 13:4–8
1 John 4:4, 8, 18
Romans 5:5; 13:8–10
Ephesians 3:16–19
Psalm 46:1; 51:10; 107:20

I pray that out of his glorious riches he may strengthen you with power through his Spirit in your inner being, so that Christ may dwell in your hearts through faith. And I pray that you, being rooted and established in love, may have power, together with all the Lord's holy people, to grasp how wide and long and high and deep is the love of Christ, and to know this love that surpasses knowledge—that you may be filled to the measure of all the fullness of God. (Ephesians 3:16–19)

At one time in my life, I believed that I was walking in the God kind of love, but the Holy Spirit opened the Word of God up to me. It revealed to me that I was not as loving and as lovable as I thought I was. Scriptures help us to understand that God's ways are truly not our ways. I realized that in order for us to walk in and operate in God's love, we must first acknowledge, know, and understand what the God kind of love is and what his love is meant to be. If we were to size ourselves up with the definition of love in and through God's Word and his meaning of love, we would live in victory more often than in defeat because God's love never fails (1 Corinthians 13:8).

Too often, we believe that love is for weak people and wimps but not so. A fearless person is one who walks in love, no matter what. He or she is not afraid to love because that perfect love has no fear; mature love has no fear.

> There is no fear in love. But perfect love drives out fear, because fear has to do with punishment. The one who fears is not made perfect in love. (1 John 4:18)

The Bible says, fear has torment but with the power of God's perfect love, we don't have to be fearful when operating in God's love. With God's powerful, perfect love, we can face anything, any person, or any situation. There are misconceptions of a person walking in love. People walking in love are not weak, fearful, timid, or pushovers. I will say this again: one of the greatest and most powerful persons to ever have lived was Jesus Christ, and he continuously walked in the God kind of love. Walking in love is not always easy either, but it is rewarding and worth it. It takes strength to walk in love. A person operating in God's love is someone who is courageous and someone who has self-control. Being able to walk in love takes being secured in who we are and holding our peace in the midst of confusion, trouble, and difficult times. A person demonstrating love is someone who can walk in forgiveness toward people who are deliberately trying to hurt that person and cause pain.

Christian love is one of the highest forms of spiritual warfare. This is why God commands and reminds us to walk in it. People operating in God's love will not wimp out under pressure. When someone mistreats people who operate in God's love, they won't retaliate because they know and understand that their inner human will be strengthened to operate in God's love and God's power of forgiveness. People who walk in God's love will stand up for the truth and tell the truth in love, while knowing and believing that God's love will protect them. A wimp would not and could not allow people to strip them naked in front of their community, hang them on a cross/tree, and kill them for something they did not do. That type of situation would take supernatural strength to handle. It would take the God kind of love to stand in all that.

If Jesus had wanted to, he could have come down off that cross and whipped, even killed a lot of his accusers and abusers. Most of us don't realize that God's love has supernatural strength that empowers us with supernatural abilities. This kind of love allows you to forgive someone who opposes you every chance they get, just because they can or want to. This kind of love allows you to give until it hurt to someone who spitefully uses you because you trust in, rely on, and look to God's love to reward you down the road for what you have done.

Love is the foundation of all things that are godly. Without love, you have nothing, and because God is love, without God, you have nothing. Not only is love a spiritual force and God's presence but love is also a choice and an action. If we choose to walk in love, we will open up to God's Spirit. When we walk in love, we walk in God, his power, his characteristics, and his anointing. God showed his love to us by dying on the cross/tree for sins he did not commit. God came down from heaven in bodily form, Jesus Christ, and bore our sins, curses, and sickness and miserable, filthy condition so that we may have an abundant life and eventually eternal life. Now that's love! God did not have to do that, but he chose to do so because of his love for humanity, his creation.

Love Language

In the Hebrew language, there are three languages for love. These love languages are different in meaning for the term *love*. *Raya*, which basically means friend, is the first word used to describe love in the Hebrew language (Song of Songs 4:7), Song of Solomon 4:7. In Song of Songs, raya is also known as companion, best friend, and/or soul mate. *Ahav*, the root word of ahava, is the second term in Hebrew for love, which means deep affection, committed or devoted love. Ahav love is more about giving love than receiving devoted love (Song of Songs 8:7), Song of Solomon 8:7. Finally, the third Hebrew term for love is *dod*, meaning to show passion, or romantic feelings; it's physical, sexual in nature. Dod also means to fondle or caress (Song of Songs 1:2), Song of Solomon 1:2.

The Three Dimension of Love

The first dimension of love is *agape*. It is a Greek term that best describes the God kind of love. It is the purest form of love, which is a divine love. Agape is the gift of love that God has for humanity. It is not characterized by desires, attractions, or needs.

Philia, the second dimension of love, is characterized as friendship or brotherly love, which humans desire and give to each other.

Love of desire or of a sexual nature is known as *eros*. Eros is the third dimension of love, which is mainly physical (Bowden and Richardson 1983, 341–342).

Not only are there three dimensions of love, but there also are several forms or types of love. When we say we love, we can mean any number of different things. In 1973-74, a Canadian named John Lee developed a widely cited approach to love. Lee suggested that there were six styles of love:

Eros—love of beauty, powerful physical attraction, and sexual desire

Mania—obsessive love, jealousy, possessiveness, and intense love dependency

Ludus—playful love, carefree quality, casualness; fun-and-games approach

Storge—companionate love, peaceful and affectionate love, based on mutual trust and respect

Agape—altruistic love, self sacrificing, kind and patient love, God's kind of love, divine love

Pragma—practical love, sensible and realistic love (Benokraitis 1996, 119)

After viewing the different dimensions and types or forms of love, let us look again at what God's Word says about love. In 1 Corinthians 13:4–8, the Word says that love is patient; love is kind. It does not envy; it does not boast; it is not proud. It is not rude; it is not self-seeking; it is not easily angered; and it keeps no record of wrongs. Love does not delight in evil but rejoice with the truth. It always protects, always trusts, always hopes, and always perseveres. Love never fails. Wow! The love of God is really something. Now, if we were to carefully read God's definition of love and be very truthful with ourselves, we would have to admit that we all have issues to work on concerning our love walks.

One day, as my husband and I had this big argument about something stupid, in which I learned a lesson about love. The Holy Spirit, the third person of the Trinity, can teach you about the things of God and teach you about you and where you are—if you allow him to. The Trinity, the Godhead, as we know him, is one God in three persons: Father, Son, and Holy Spirit.

Anyway, I had a self-righteous approach to judging my husband. I told him that I knew what love was and that I walked in love toward him but that he did not walk in love toward me. Well, the very next day, I went to meet him after work to continue the argument, for intense fellowship, and to fight. While I was waiting in my car for him to get off from work to continue verbally fighting, I had the audacity to read 1 Corinthians 13:1–8, known as the "love chapter." How arrogant and self righteous was that of me to sit there reading the Word of God with the attitude of being right, to argue my point of view instead of walking in love toward my husband?

As I read the Word of God, the Holy Spirit began to convict me about my love walk. Reading down the list of the God kind of love, I could do nothing but repent and drive off. The love of God does not disrespect or get upset easily.

> It does not dishonor others, it is not self-seeking, it is not easily angered, it keeps no record of wrongs. Love does not delight in evil but rejoices with the truth. (1 Corinthians 13:5–6)

Well, on those two Bible verses alone, I was busted right there on the spot. So I kindly packed my Bible up and drove home, fixed my family dinner, and let the argument go. Mark 11:25 says, "Whenever you stand praying, if you have anything against anyone, forgive him [drop the issue; let it go], so that your Father who is in heaven will also forgive you your transgressions and wrongdoings [against him and others]" (AMP). At that time, after reading the Word, the Holy Spirit really convicted me. I was so bent on being right and not operating in God's love, as the righteousness of God would lead us to do so. Ever since that day, the Holy Spirit has taught me a lesson in love, as the Word of

God also spoke with me regarding my love walk. I realized that I had to cry out to God and ask him to teach me how to love. When we realize that we need help from God the Father, he is right there, ready and willing to assist us in true love. So many people are able to help us but are not willing. God, however, is able and willing to help us in our love walks and anything else we may lay down before him, anytime. The Word says that he is a very present helper in our time of need. "God is our refuge and strength [mighty and impenetrable], a very present and well-proved help in trouble" (Psalm 46:1 AMP). Are you willing and ready to obey what he has already instructed you to do; that is, walk in his love? Romans 5:5 remind us that God "has poured out his love into our heart by the Holy Spirit, whom he has given us."

Our ways seem right to us, but God wants us to learn his way of doing things. Believe it or not, God is wiser and smarter than we are. His Word, the Bible, is filled with truth and direction for our lives, if we would just submit to its authority. If we are truly wise, we will come to understand that we need to check in with the one who created us. Let the spirit of wisdom minister to you through reading the Word and prayer. Most important, we need to stop examining ourselves against human standards and examine ourselves (our hearts and minds) through the Word of God. We need to examine ourselves and look through the mirror of God's Word.

> Create in me a pure heart, O God and renew a steadfast spirit within me. (Psalm 51:10)

> He sent out his word and healed them;
> he rescued them from the grave. (Psalm
> 107:20)

God's help is available to assist us in our love walks, but we must be willing to cry out for help and ask him to teach us how to walk in his love, his way. The only way we will be able to walk in the God kind of love is by one experience and example at a time. The perfect example of God's love has been demonstrated to us through the person of Jesus Christ. While we were sinners and enemies of God, Christ died for us on the cross.

> But God demonstrates his own love for us
> in this: While we were still sinners, Christ
> died for us. (Romans 5:8)

Remember that practice makes perfect. Practice your love walk. The only way God will teach us how to walk in his love is through practice. Every day of your life, you have a chance to practice how to walk in the God kind of love. Are you going to continue to live and handle things like the natural man, the old man, your old self, who does not want to ever give up? The sinner man, the old man, will try to keep rising to the top and handle things, but you have to be diligent in walking in the truth of God's love and his righteousness. The choice to love will always be yours—your choice, your life that God has blessed you with to demonstrate his love.

The only way in which God will teach us how to love is by one experience at a time. Every day, you and I are faced with opportunities to walk in the God kind of love or to walk in our own strengths, power, and abilities. The only way we will learn to love like God is if we choose to love like him. We are called to walk in love. God, however, has not called us to be doormats for people who just walk all over us or to allow ourselves to be treated any kind of way. As children of God, we have the Holy Spirit, and we know when we are walking in love or not. Remember that when we walk in God's love, we walk in God's power and his strength because greater is he that is in us, than he that is in the world (1 John 4:4). God did not create us to be foolish people either. A person who walks in the God kind of love is not foolish or a pushover.

Because of the supernatural strength of God's love, we will be able to stand with power and authority in a hard place and deal with difficult people without being bitter or nasty but continue to operate from a place of power and authority, demonstrating the power of God's love.

Three

Hello, Judas; Goodbye, Pain

Genesis 29:31; 50:19–20
Deuteronomy 30:19–20
Isaiah 54:17; 61:7
Psalm 75:6–7
Romans 8:31
Hebrew 4:15
Corinthians 3:18
John 13:21, 27
3 John 1:2–3

There will be times when we all experience betrayal by someone very close to us. Any act of betrayal will always be painful and devastating at first, but as time moves on, we must learn to pick up the fragments and what's left and continue on our life's journeys. During different stages of one's life, one may encounter someone around operating in the spirit of Judas. Who was Judas? He was the one who ultimately betrayed Christ. He was one of the twelve disciples who were close to Jesus, eating with him, listening to his teaching, and even staying with him as he ministered from town to town.

People who are Judas will be there, lurking around you, pretending and trying to act as if they are there for you, but they are not because they are fake. The deceitful spirit of Judas will try to act as if they love and support you, but they can't. The Judas spirit is not really for you.

Please note that someone with the Judas spirit may be hanging around you, but remember they are not for you, nor are they with you. Someone operating in the Judas spirit is sent by Satan to kill, steal, destroy, or sabotage the promises, blessings, and plans of God for your life.

The spirit of Judas is deceitful and disruptive. A number of people don't realize that they have yielded to the spirit of Judas and are operating in a demonic assignment against and toward their brothers and sisters in the body of Christ. They don't understand that they are destroying or trying to destroy someone's assignment or purpose in life.

The spirit of Judas can only operate through someone who has yielded to demonic oppression and someone who is harboring ill feelings, such as jealousy, envy, strife, and hatred. When we are quick to release ill feelings, the Spirit of the living God and the power of his love can then flow through us. The Holy Spirit tries to reveal things to us when there is something off in our spirits that we need to address. But if we are not in tune with the Holy Spirit, we ignore God in our lives and yield to Satan. Yielding to Satan and his counsel, however, opens the door to ill feelings, like the spirit of Judas, which takes root and grows in our spirits, if allowed. Just as love is a spiritual force that God uses to empower us, Judas is also a spiritual force that the enemy uses to destroy the lives of others and, eventually, the life of the person operating in the demonic spirit of betrayal—the Judas spirit.

A lot of times, Judas will try to go with us to the next level and stop the move of God in our lives, but he cannot. Hatred, deceitfulness, and any other kind of evilness cannot stand to be around when the presence of God is near. Promotion to the next level is possible and can happen for you. Remember that true promotion comes from God and him only. The Bible says,

> For promotion cometh neither from the east, nor from the west, nor from the south. But God is the judge: he putteth down one, and setteth up another. (Psalm 75:6–7 KJV)

Wherever the Lord is, there is the presence of love because God is love. God loves us so much that he desires to promote us from where we are to another level in him. He also desires to promote us in the natural with knowledge and wisdom. God desires that we understand:

> Beloved, I pray that you may prosper in all things and be in health, just as your soul prospers. (3 John 1:2 NKJV)

Now that's promotion in every area of life.

Love is again a powerful force, a spiritual force that brings promotion in every area of one's life. The spirit of love is the actual presence of God, just as ill feelings and every form of evilness can usher in the presence of demonic forces.

Where God's love is in action, his goodness is there, and the presence of evil cannot be where God's goodness is because they cannot coexist. God's love always brings promotion, and evilness always brings some form of destruction. In his love, we move from glory to glory. So in God, we should be moving from glory to glory.

> And we all, who with unveiled faces contemplate the Lord's glory, are being transformed into his image with ever-increasing glory, which comes from the Lord, who is the Spirit. (2 Corinthians 3:18 NIV)

Jesus was our perfect example because he demonstrated in the flesh what we are supposed to be doing. As the glory of God moved in Jesus' life, his promotion was at hand, and some of the Jewish leaders desired to kill him. The Jewish leaders desired to kill him because they could not stand to see Jesus promoted, and rise above them in any way. They were extremely jealous of Christ Jesus. The Jewish leaders had ill feelings because they had the spirit of Judas.

Please note: you don't have to spend time worrying or trying to figure out who Judas is in your life because the power of God's love will always reveal and expose who's who in our lives, as the Holy Spirit gives us the spirit of discernment. The Holy Spirit, our helper, will show us who is for us and who is not. Love is a spirit, and the Word of God tells us in 1 John that God is love. There is nothing hidden from the Spirit of God and the power of his love.

Let us look at the encounter between Jesus and Judas

right before the ultimate betrayal. Jesus knew when his betrayal would happen and who would betray him because the power of God's love flowing through him had revealed it to him. Even in the midst of what was about to happen, Jesus operated in love toward Judas. He did not try to harm or hurt Judas in any way. We must understand that revenge belongs to God. Too often, we waste time and energy trying to hurt people and get back at them for the wrong they have done to us. Jesus looks at Judas and tells him to do whatever he has to do quickly.

> After [Judas had taken] the piece of bread,
> Satan entered him. Then Jesus said to him,
> "What you are going to do, do quickly
> [without delay]." (John 13:27 AMP).

Jesus was able to operate in power and authority because he kept himself available and open to God's love. He did not allow Judas to steal his focus from what God was calling him to do. Please remember that we can't be distracted by people who mean us no good. Forgive them, stay focused, and keep operating in your God-given purpose. Once Judas is revealed to you, don't allow him to steal your focus. Stay focused on what you have to do, and keep promoting God in your life.

> And those he predestined, he also called;
> those he called, he also justified; those he
> justified, he also glorified. What, then, shall
> we say in response to these things? If God
> is for us, who can be against us? (Romans
> 8:30–31)

We have to know that God is for us. As a matter of fact, God is so much for promoting his children that he will even use Judas to help promote his children to the next level.

Look at the story of Joseph and his brothers and how they hated him and treated him badly. They even sought to kill him. Joseph's brothers thought they were hurting him, but they helped move him in the plan and purposes of God for his life. At the end of the book of Genesis 50, Joseph told his brothers not to be scared of being in the position of needing him, now that their father, Jacob, was dead. But what they meant to hurt Joseph with, God used to prepare him to be a blessing to many. Afterward, God promoted Joseph to the next level, in the spirit and in the natural.

> When Joseph's brothers saw that their father was dead, they said, "What if Joseph carries a grudge against us and pays us back in full for all the wrong which we did to him?" So they sent word to Joseph, saying, "Your father commanded us before he died, saying, 'You are to say to Joseph, "I beg you, please forgive the transgression of your brothers and their sin, for they did you wrong." Now, please forgive the transgression of the servants of the God of your father." And Joseph wept when they spoke to him. Then his brothers went and fell down before him [in confession]; then they said, "Behold, we are your servants (slaves)." But Joseph said to them, "Do not be afraid, for am I in the place of God?

[Vengeance is His, not mine.] As for you, you meant evil against me, but God meant it for good in order to bring about this present outcome, that many people would be kept alive [as they are this day]. So now, do not be afraid; I will provide for you and support you and your little ones." So he comforted them [giving them encouragement and hope] and spoke [with kindness] to their hearts. (Genesis 50:14–21 AMP)

Joseph was able to bless those who hurt him because of three reasons: first, he knew God; second, he loved and honored God; and third, he was able to forgive his brothers because he trusted God. And not only did he trust God, but he trusted God for his life. It's so awesome how God can turn hatred and negativity around that was intended to destroy someone's life. The Word of God states, "And we know that in all things God works for the good of those who love him, who have been called according to his purpose" (Romans 8:28 NIV). That is just what can happen for you. God can take whatever people meant to hurt you with and turn it around to bless many, as well as you.

But we must let the power of God's love have its way in our lives. Don't retaliate; don't try to get back at people who lie to you or manipulate, play games, and try to destroy and hurt you—just pure evil. Learn to trust in God's love and leave these types of people in God's hands. Joseph hurt by people who were close to him, but he chose to trust God, forgive, and love those who had hurt him. Jesus was also hurt by many but chose to forgive and love those who hurt him.

Jesus felt pain and hurt, just like you and I have experienced. The Word says we have a high priest who went through the same things we go through, but he sinned not (Hebrews 4:15). Jesus was truthful with himself, the inner man—that's why he could walk in forgiveness. The forgiveness Jesus walked in kept his spirit-man clean of ill feelings, ill emotions, and ill spirits so that the love of God and the power of God could flow through him.

We cannot harbor ill feelings, emotions, and spirits and expect a major move of God on our behalf. The Holy Spirit, the Spirit of the living God on the inside of us, is very sensitive to any ill feelings, emotions, pain, and hurt. And when we harbor ill spirits, it affects our love walks. Learn to examine yourself daily for any ill spirits, and repent. Get yourself together so that God's love may flow through you. Be truthful with God; release and submit all ill feelings in the spirit to him, so that he can replace it with his love and his peace.

Jesus was able to move on with life because he did not allow himself to get stuck in the Judas experience. At one point, we will have to decide if we are going to continue in life or die in a dead relationship and get stuck in our Judas experiences. Let's face it—there are some people in our lives for a particular reason; some are there to derail us, distract us, or destroy our lives. But some people are in our lives only for a particular reason and season to bless and help us in God's purpose/plan for our lives. We mess up when we try to hold on to something or someone when it is time to move on in our life journeys. If we move toward the perfect will of God, we must realize that we are on a journey heading somewhere. In the midst of our journeys heading somewhere, we will experience different things and different people.

God created you and me for a particular purpose and plan in life. On the journey of life, we will encounter all types of things: roadblocks, detours, traffic jams, wrong directions, accidents, and all types of trouble, problems, and people. However, no experience whatever that we encounter should be able to stop us from our journey because the Word of God reminds us that if God is for us, who can be against us?

> And those whom He predestined, He also called; and those whom He called, He also justified [declared free of the guilt of sin]; and those whom He justified, He also glorified [raising them to a heavenly dignity]. What then shall we say to all these things? If God is for us who can be [successful] against us? (Romans 8:30–31 AMP)

Well, God is for us, and his love is waiting to empower us for life's journey. We must understand and realize what the scripture says:

> "No weapon that is formed against you will succeed; and every tongue that rises against you in judgment you will condemn. This [peace, righteousness, security, and triumph over opposition] is the heritage of the servants of the Lord, and this is their vindication from Me" says the Lord. (Isaiah 54:17 AMP)

As a matter of fact, after Judas has been expose to us and the betrayal has been committed against us, we should look for a promotion. Our promotion will sometime be in the spiritual realm, the natural realm or both. Again, God's Word reminds us that when we trust God and his love, we can walk in wealth and health, as our souls prosper. God will give us double for our trouble, if we're willing to move on in the spirit of love.

After an encounter with Judas, if we ever learn the art of forgiveness, our healing process will happen quicker than we could imagine. If we ever learn to release people from the pain, insults, and injuries that may have caused us hurt, we will move on with our lives for the better. So many of us are looking for Judas to come to us and ask us for forgiveness, but most times, it will never happen. And in some cases, it cannot happen for several reasons—due to a death or perhaps relocation. Sometimes it's just not in some people to acknowledge that they have wronged you. It is very important, however, for us to be healed. In such cases as these, we must rely on and turn to our God for healing. Also, during those times, it is very important to release the pain, the hurt, and move on with our lives, no matter what. Our healing, soundness, and wholeness should not be in the hands of Judas type of people anyway because he comes to kill, steal, and destroy our lives.

Stop giving Judas the power to heal you; he can't. It's impossible for Judas to help or heal you because he is a destroyer. He is on the enemy's side. Some healing is supernatural and only God—and those he sends our way with the healing power to operate through them—can heal certain places in our lives. Believe me, God knows, and he is waiting and wanting to help and heal us, but we must acknowledge and turn to him. God knows all about it.

In Genesis 29:31, only God could heal a woman named Leah. "When the Lord saw that Leah was not loved, he opened her womb." When love hurts, what do you do? Turn to God for a supernatural healing. In the midst of the Judas experiences, God will see our pain and do something very special for us, but we must turn from the pain to a healing and loving God to receive it. When we say, "Hello, Judas, I forgive you," the love of God comes in and says goodbye to the pain. Once we say goodbye to the pain, we can say welcome to a glorious future. Which one do you want? We can't have both. While reaching for our healing, we must let go of the pain. If we hold to the pain, we can't embrace our healing. The choice is ours; God will not make the decision for us.

We have the will to choose. God has set before us two open doors. Which one will you choose—blessings or curses? Judas and pain or healing and blessings? The choice will always be ours (Deuteronomy 30:19–20).

Four

Danger! The Absence of Self Love

Numbers 23:19
Leviticus 19:18
Matthew 22:39
Mark 12:30–31
Hebrew 12:1–2
Galatians 5:20
Jeremiah 18:3; 29:11
Psalm 139:14
2 Timothy 1:7
1 Peter 5:7
1 John 4:18

You shall not take revenge nor bear any grudge against the sons of your people, but you shall love your neighbor (acquaintance, associate, companion) as yourself; I am the Lord. (Leviticus 19:18 AMP)

> The second is like it, "You shall love your neighbor as yourself [that is, unselfishly seek the best or higher good for others]." (Matthew 22:39)

Our society has major problems and much hurt because it is filled with people who cannot love one another. They cannot love others because they don't love themselves. The truth of the matter is that people don't know how to love others, nor do they know how to practice self-love. If we knew how to practice self-love and self-care, we could love others as we love ourselves. Of course, there are a lot of selfish people in the world who are concerned only about themselves and their needs. But just because people are selfish or self-centered does not necessarily mean that they love themselves. Self-love goes much deeper than just getting what one wants or desires to satisfy the natural man, and it goes deeper than just having one's own way. We know that selfishness is not of God. Selfishness is not one of the by-products of the fruit of the spirit, love, but of the flesh.

> Now the practices of the sinful nature are clearly evident: they are sexual immorality, impurity, sensuality (total irresponsibility, lack of self-control), idolatry, sorcery, hostility, strife, jealousy, fits of anger, disputes, dissensions, factions [that promote heresies], envy, drunkenness, riotous behavior, and other things like these. I warn you beforehand, just as I did previously, that those who practice such things will

not inherit the kingdom of God. But the fruit of the Spirit [the result of His presence within us] is love [unselfish concern for others], joy, [inner] peace, patience [not the ability to wait, but how we act while waiting], kindness, goodness, faithfulness, gentleness, self-control. Against such things there is no law. And those who belong to Christ Jesus have crucified the sinful nature together with its passions and appetites. If we [claim to] live by the [Holy] Spirit, we must also walk by the Spirit [with personal integrity, godly character, and moral courage—our conduct empowered by the Holy Spirit]. We must not become conceited, challenging or provoking one another, envying one another. (Galatians 5:19–26 AMP)

To be selfish is to oppose the nature of God. Now that's arrogant—to oppose the very one who is responsible for our existence, who created us. To be selfish, according to *Webster's Dictionary*, is to be "concerned only or primarily with oneself without regard for others." According to this definition, selfish people will not love their neighbor as themselves because they are wrapped up in themselves, and selfishness is no representation of true love anyway. It would be impossible because selfish people have no regard for anyone but themselves. So selfishness is not and does not represent self-love. For this reason, most of us have been taught that self-love is wrong. Self-love is not wrong, but selfishness is; they are two different things. One can have self-love and not be selfish, but selfishness is being consumed only with self, and that is not of God. As previously stated, God is love, and he so loved us that he gave to us out of his abundance. He keeps on giving to us, supplying our needs—spiritual and physical needs.

However, true love—the God kind of love—does not insist on having its own way. True love for self is actually being aware of the Creator's love for you and accepting who he created you to be. Those who practice self-love are aware of their strengths as well as their weaknesses and all in between. They will accept the good, the bad, and the unique about themselves. If anything should arise that becomes challenging to their self-existence, they will deal with it most positively. If self-loving people find themselves struggling with the issue of life, they understand that they can seek and ultimately find help from the one who created them. They will look to the one who gave them life and take instruction from the owner's manual (God the Father and his Word). Those who love themselves will constantly go down to the "potter's house," or look into the Word for assistance, and allow God to work on them (Jeremiah 18:3).

We all are a work in progress. God took pleasure in creating us; now let him take pleasure in shaping our lives. King David said, "For I am fearfully and wonderfully made" (Psalm 139:14). When life seems to tell you that you are not significant and that you don't matter, remind yourself that you were fearfully and wonderfully made, King David said. Who are you to argue with God?

God the Father commanded that we love ourselves as we love others. Most of us do not realize how often we break this commandment to love our neighbors as we love ourselves.

> And you shall love the Lord your God with all your heart, and with all your soul (life), and with all your mind (thought, understanding), and with all your strength.' This is the second: "you shall [unselfishly] [a love your neighbor as yourself.' There is no other commandment greater than these." (Mark 12:30–31 AMP)

Most of us work on loving others, but we overlook this very important part of scripture: "Love thy neighbor as you love yourself." When we do not love ourselves, it is a slap in God's face because he said that we are fearfully and wonderfully made. Our Father, God, took pleasure in creating us. Too often, we allow society and others to tell us what is beautiful and what is acceptable.

Friend, what does God say about you that you need to be concerned with? If you are going to be empowered, you must start loving yourself through the eyes of God and his Word. It will change your life. Stop being consumed with what others say, and think about you. God does not care if you are fat, skinny, short, tall, rich, poor, yellow, brown, male, female, hairy, bald, blind, crippled, or crazy. When you do not practice self-love (not selfishness); you don't honor God. When you do not accept who you really are and were created to be, you tell God the Father that you know more than he does. You honor the God of the universe, who created everything and who knows all things, by loving yourself. Not loving yourself is a slap in the face of God; you are actually saying that you know what is best for your life. My friend that is a dangerous place to be, saying you know better than God and what's best for your life. Thinking you know more than God is a form of pride. God knew what he was doing when he created you just the way you are.

Believe it or not, when we constantly focus on ourselves and what's right or wrong with us, what we are practicing idolatry. Danger! Danger! There we go again, messing up by focusing on and being consumed by the wrong stuff. Stop right where you are and just thank God for giving you life. God could have let another seed be born instead of you. The Word of God tells us,

> Therefore, since we are surrounded by so great a cloud of witnesses [who by faith have testified to the truth of God's absolute faithfulness], stripping off every unnecessary weight and the sin which so easily and cleverly entangles us, let us run with endurance and active persistence the race that is set before us, [looking away from all that will distract us and] focusing our eyes on Jesus, who is the Author and Perfecter of faith [the first incentive for our belief and the One who brings our faith to maturity], who for the joy [of accomplishing the goal] set before Him endured the cross, disregarding the shame, and sat down at the right hand of the throne of God [revealing

His deity, His authority, and the completion
of His work]. (Hebrews 12:1–2 AMP)

The enemy of God, Satan, wants you and me to be consumed with things that don't matter, so that we won't live the blessed life that God has so gracefully blessed us with. Life is always something good to thank God for. God said everything he made was good. Begin to accept who you really are. Practice self-love because God tells us that he knows the plans he has for us and the purpose—the reason why he created us.

> "For I know the plans and thoughts that
> I have for you,' says the Lord, 'plans for
> peace and well-being and not for disaster,
> to give you a future and a hope." (Jeremiah
> 29:11 AMP)

So what if certain people don't like or care for you? God thought enough of you to create you and allowed you to be born out of nothing; as the Bible says, from the dust of the earth. I know it is important for us to live in peace with all people. Unfortunately, sometimes that may not be possible. But that should be our aim and plan—to live in peace with everyone. From King David to Jesus, they honored God the Father by accepting who they were and who they were created to be. The Pharisees and Sadducees were conservative religious leaders who only accepted the written Law of Moses. In Jesus' day, the Pharisees and Sadducees came upon him to intimidate him and tried to humiliate him, telling him who he was and was not. Jesus, however, was not having any of it. Each time Jesus did not allow the Pharisees and Sadducees to mistreat him or tell him who he was and his purpose in life, they became upset with him. He reminded them each time that he was the Son of God and that he was about his Father's business and his will.

Friend, stop allowing people, society, and this world to tell you who you are and why you were created. If you want to know who you are, ask God. If you want to know your purpose in this life, ask God because the Holy Spirit will show and teach you all things. The Word of God says if you need to know anything, ask God, and the Holy Spirit will teach you all things. People may not like you or accept you for who you are and were created to be. We are to look to God anyway because he created us.

The following two scriptures come to mind when we are seeking answers from God:

> If any of you lacks wisdom [to guide him through a decision or circumstance], he is to ask of [our benevolent] God, who gives to everyone generously and without rebuke or blame, and it will be given to him. But he must ask [for wisdom] in faith, without doubting [God's willingness to help], for the one who doubts is like a billowing surge of the sea that is blown about and tossed by the wind. (James 1:5–6 AMP)

> "For God has unveiled them and revealed them to us through the [Holy] Spirit; for the Spirit searches all things [diligently], even

[sounding and measuring] the [profound] depths of God [the divine counsels and things far beyond human understanding]."
(1 Corinthians 2:10 AMP)

Those who operate in self-love will seek God and pursue God to find out why and for what purpose God created them. Stop going to everyone, trying to figure out why you were created. Remember that only God truly knows why you were created. Also keep in mind that if you lack knowledge in anything, you can ask our heavenly Father. Ask him to reveal your purpose and destiny to you. He is faithful and will reveal to you who you are, but you must seek him through prayer and through meditating on his Word. God sometimes will send someone to confirm what he has already revealed to you, but so often, you don't hear the voice of God because you are listening and looking to everyone else for answers.

Those who do not practice self-love will spend their entire lives trying to do and be something they were not created to be. I'm not talking about dreams and aspirations—we all have them. I think, though, that some of us just don't trust God with our hopes and dreams. Then the spirit of pride comes in, and those same people will wear out themselves or others, trying to impress people they don't even like or even care for. What is all this for, except to project a false image?

My friend, you must be real with yourself and get a life. If you love yourself, you cannot be a person who is living a lie. If you love yourself, be truthful with yourself and be truthful with God. Lies cannot exist in the midst of true love. Those who are living a lie cannot rejoice in the truth of

God. Love rejoices in the truth. And God is truth; he cannot lie. God is also love, and lies cannot coexist with love.

> God has said that he is not a man that he shall lie, has he not spoken and it comes to pass. (Numbers 23:19)

If individuals do not have self-love, they cannot rejoice in the truth of God. Therefore, anyone who does not have self-love will live a miserable life. A miserable life is a life without God the Father, the one who created you out of love. You will live a life as an impostor if you don't practice self-love. Living as an impostor, you will hurt people, causing pain to everyone with whom you come in contact.

At this point, it would be impossible for people to love their neighbors as themselves because they don't love themselves. They do not know what love is. In order to give love, one must know what it is. And if you don't love yourself, you will not love others. Get to know yourself; you might come to love yourself. For so many people, it is difficult to accept and deal with things concerning themselves, but with God's love, they can do it. The worst thing for any of us to do is to avoid things we don't necessarily like about ourselves. We don't realize that to avoid something does not make it go away. To avoid something is a sign of fear, "but God did not give us a spirit of fear, but of power, love and a sound mind" (2 Timothy 1:7).

The Word of God reminds us that perfect love, the God kind of love, casts out fear (1 John 4:18). We have nothing to fear about ourselves and why we were created. With the power of God's love and with the help of the Holy Spirit, we can face anything.

It's OK to practice self-love through the eyes of God. Ask God to help you to be true to yourself and deal with what you are trying to avoid. If you seek his help, he will help you because he created you out of the abundance of his love.

Remember what the Word says: "Casting all your cares [all your anxieties, all your worries, and all your concerns, once and for all] on Him, for He cares about you [with deepest affection, and watches over you very carefully]" (1 Peter 5:7 AMP).

Five

For If They Knew Better, They Would Do Better (How to Forgive When It Hurts)

1 Corinthians 13:4–8

1John 4:4, 8, 18

Mark 12:28–34

Matthew 22:37

Romans 5:2–5; 13:8–10

Galatians 5:6, 13, 21-23

Leviticus 19:18

Ephesians 3:16–19

Psalm 51:10; 107:20

Proverbs 4:23

The Power of Love

True Love, the God Kind of Love

> You shall not take revenge nor bear any
> grudge against the sons of your people, but
> you shall love your neighbor (acquaintance,
> associate, and companion) as yourself; I am
> the Lord. (Leviticus 19:18 AMP)

What is love? According to the Word of God, love is several
different things, but it is constant and steadfast during
difficult times. I believe we have a good picture of what
true love is in 1 Corinthians:

> If I speak with the tongues of men and
> of angels, but have not love [for others
> growing out of God's love for me], then I
> have become only a noisy gong or a clanging
> cymbal [just an annoying distraction]. And
> if I have the gift of prophecy [and speak a
> new message from God to the people], and
> understand all mysteries, and [possess] all
> knowledge; and if I have all [sufficient] faith
> so that I can remove mountains, but do
> not have love [reaching out to others], I am
> nothing. If I give all my possessions to feed
> the poor, and if I surrender my body to be
> burned, but do not have love, it does me no
> good at all. Love endures with patience and
> serenity, love is kind and thoughtful, and is
> not jealous or envious; love does not brag

and is not proud or arrogant. It is not rude; it is not self-seeking, it is not provoked [nor overly sensitive and easily angered]; it does not take into account a wrong endured. It does not rejoice at injustice, but rejoices with the truth [when right and truth prevail]. Love bears all things [regardless of what comes], believes all things [looking for the best in each one], hopes all things [remaining and endures all things [without weakening]. Love never fails [it never fades nor ends]." But as for prophecies, they will pass away; as for tongues, they will cease; as for the gift of special knowledge, it will pass away. (1 Corinthians 13:4–8 AMP)

I believe God is calling us to a radical love walk, regardless of where we are and what we have to face in this life. The Word of God tells us that God poured his abundant love in our hearts through the Holy Spirit, while we were in the midst of a helpless and difficult state, and because of his love in our hearts, we have access to the ultimate power and authority of God through his love in this life. The love that God has for us is so awesome that nothing can stop his love from reaching us—no pain or suffering. Hallelujah, I can't stop praising God the Father for his unfailing love. It's so encouraging.

Through Him we also have access by faith into this [remarkable state of] grace in which we [firmly and safely and securely] stand. Let us rejoice in our hope and the confident assurance of [experiencing and enjoying] the glory of [our great] God [the manifestation of His excellence and power]. And not only this, but [with joy] let us exult in our sufferings and rejoice in our hardships, knowing that hardship (distress, pressure, trouble) produces patient endurance; and endurance, proven character (spiritual maturity); and proven character, hope and confident assurance [of eternal salvation]. Such hope [in God's promises] never disappoints us, because God's love has been abundantly poured out within our hearts through the Holy Spirit who was given to us. (Romans 5:2–5 AMP)

Now that we have an idea of what love is, let's look at what love is not: it is not manipulation, deceit, hate, jealousy, or envy. Love has no strife; it is not harsh or brutal; it does not control or rebel. It has no discord and is not cruel, greedy, disloyal, unfaithful, or selfish. Love is a spirit, and the Bible says that God is love (1 John 4:8).

Almighty God, the Spirit of love—his presence has power and authority. As we allow the power of God's love to flow through our lives, we can experience joy and excitement for living. Like the old song says, "This joy that I have, the world did not give it to me, and the world cannot take it away." Well, this love that I have, the world did not give it to me, and it sure can't take it away. The love of God will always bring victorious living. When we become aware of God's love, it will bring us an unexplainable sense of peace. So many people don't have a zeal for living. They just go through life, existing from one day to the next, simply because they do not realize how much God loves them and how much he wants his love to flow in and through them.

God's love is one of the first spiritual gifts to humanity, but most of us do not acknowledge the depth of God's love, simply because we don't realize that it is a spiritual force with power, anointing, and abilities. And because we have not acknowledged God's love, we cannot operate in God's power and the authority he has given us on earth. We need to give up our hang-ups, get together, and serve God and each other through the spiritual force of love. We must understand that when we are not loving but are scheming, plotting, backbiting, or harboring jealousy and hatred toward each other—just to name a few—the kingdom of darkness advances in our lives and in the earthly realm. But if we learn to walk in God's love, the kingdom of heaven advances.

One quick question: whose side are you on? Let's get together on kingdom business and work on bringing the kingdom of God here on earth. When we don't walk in God's love, his spiritual force, we are working against him and his kingdom. Either we are for God—by walking in his love, his spirit, and his force—or we are working for Satan, harboring ill feelings and operating in evilness. Quick question again: whose side are you on?

The fruit of the Spirit is love. A good example of walking in God's love is in Galatians 5:22–23. We are reminded of what the fruit of the Spirit is and what it will produce if we walk in it; in other words, if we cultivate the love of God in our lives. We have to cultivate our love walks daily. We cultivate our love through prayer and learning and knowing the Word of God. Prayer helps us cultivate the fruit of the Spirit so that we may grow spiritually. Operating in God's love and practicing it also helps us to grow spiritually.

There are many forces or spirits that try to destroy us spiritually. John 10:10 says, "The thief comes only in order to steal and kill and destroy. I came that they may have and enjoy life, and have it in abundance [to the full, till it overflows]" (AMP). We must take heed of what the Word says—that the enemy, Satan, comes into our lives to kill, steal, and destroy our lives, but Jesus said that he himself comes into our lives that we may enjoy life and have it more abundantly.

God gives us the ability to love unlovable people during difficult times. Dealing with difficult people can be challenging, but we can still operate in God's love toward them and not give in to the evilness of others while in a difficult place, no matter what. Sometimes, we will face difficulties, difficult people, or hard places, situations, and circumstances, but we must remember the words of Jesus and the love of God. God wants us to win, to be victorious in life. However, while we agree with God that he loves us and wants us to win, regardless, at the same time, we are dealing with spirits of depression, heaviness, bitterness, illness, unforgiveness, infirmity, hated, anger, hopelessness, and fear. All of these spirits try to steal our joy, peace, and love. But even in the midst of difficulties and uncertainties, we can still have the presence of God, his peace, his joy, and his love with us because we have his Spirit, the Holy Spirit, living inside us. The evidence of his presence is with us through the Holy Spirit versus the sinful nature (Galatians 5:13–25). If we say that we belong to Christ, then we have crucified the lust of the flesh, our sinful nature.

We must find our way back to love. Our old nature, however, our flesh, does not want to operate in God's love. The evidence of God's love has the power to bring us into submission to himself and in line with his spirit. The fruit of the Spirit, love, will produce joy, peace, patience, kindness, goodness, faithfulness, gentleness, and self-control (Galatians 5:22–23). Everything that God the Father wanted to teach us is based wholly on love—God's love for us, our love for him, our love for each other, and our love for self. But remember that self-love is not selfishness. This is also why the Word of God reminds us that the greatest commandment to keep is to walk in love—love thy neighbor as you love yourself. Without love, we have nothing because anything absent of love is without God. God is love. The very excess of God is exemplified in love. Everything in the kingdom is based on love, and we have nothing without love, not even access to kingdom benefits and blessings.

In Matthew 22:36–40, when Jesus was being questioned about which of the commandments was the greatest, he told the religious teachers that the greatest of all commandments was to walk in love. And believe it or not, your love walk is just where your healing is—your blessings, your peace, and your prosperity, even as your soul prospers. It's all connected to your love walk.

> But if you are guided and led by the Spirit, you
> are not subject to the Law. Now the practices

of the sinful nature are clearly evident: they are sexual immorality, impurity, sensuality (total irresponsibility, lack of self-control), idolatry, sorcery, hostility, strife, jealousy, fits of anger, disputes, dissensions, factions [that promote heresies], envy, drunkenness, riotous behavior, and other things like these. I warn you beforehand, just as I did previously, that those who practice such things will not inherit the kingdom of God. But the fruit of the Spirit [the result of His presence within us] is love [unselfish concern for others], joy, [inner] peace, patience [not the ability to wait, but how we act while waiting], kindness, goodness, faithfulness, gentleness, and self-control. Against such things there is no law. And those who belong to Christ Jesus have crucified the sinful nature together with its passions and appetites. If we [claim to] live by the [Holy] Spirit, we must also walk by the Spirit [with personal integrity, godly character, and moral courage—our conduct empowered by the Holy Spirit]. We must not become conceited, challenging or provoking one another, envying one another. (Galatians 5:18–26 AMP)

Now, I ask you: how we can say that we are for God and not walk in the fruit of the Spirit, which is the power of God's love? How can we also say we know him but not practice his presence by walking in his love? When we practice love, we are practicing his presence. As we practice the fruit of the Spirit, love, and being in God's presence, we will experience other spirits, such as joy, peace, kindness, and everything that is good. The entire Word of God is summed up in a single command: love.

> Love your neighbor as yourself. (Galatians 5:14)

Again my friend, examine your love walk. If someone is walking in hatred, envy, cheating, and greed; remember that person's love walk is not right and out of order. Where is the love? Get back in line with God, and start practicing his presence by walking in love. So many of us miss out on the greatest love affair of a lifetime because we don't acknowledge God's love, and we don't operate in his love. We must examine ourselves and allow the love of God to flow in and through our lives.

By the way, God plays for keeps. He is not looking for any part-time lovers. So don't think of skipping out on God or two-timing him. It's best that you don't mess over him in any kind of way because you cannot mock God. We need to be consumed with the love of God, or leave it alone. Just as Jesus was a living example of God's love, we are to be an example of his love as well.

Our love walk is very important to our Christian walk, spiritual growth, and development. The more of God's love we walk in, the more we grow spiritual. As we walk in God's love, the evidence of his presence and power is made manifest in and through our lives. If we allow it, God's love can and will transform us. As more of the transformation of love takes place in our lives, we will become more like him. God intends for us to be transformed into his image more and more.

It is my belief that the more we yield to the spirit of love, the more we will walk in the power of God, and his presence will fill our daily lives. The power of God's love will turn our lives completely around. The Word says it is the goodness of the Lord that causes us to repent. God's goodness demonstrates his love shown toward us. This love, once experienced, will cause one to become a new person, a better person in Christ Jesus. As we allow God's love to transform us, his power will flow in and through our lives to change things for the better, which eventually will help us when things sometimes become difficult.

Our love walk will always affect our quality of life—how well and how long we live. Some people literally have died from a broken heart; they felt as though no one truly loved them. Perhaps they never experienced how to love God or themselves. Sadly, they did not come to know and understand that God's love was available to them. Love is a very important part of life. As we develop spiritually and physically, it is very important that we experience love, but most important, we need to experience God's love.

It is my belief that if someone is raised in an atmosphere of love or maybe experiences love later in life, he or she will have a healthy lifestyle. Healthy emotions and a sense of well being, I believe, are signs of someone who has experienced love and care. People who have been abused emotionally, mentally, and/or physically often are afraid to love because they don't know if they can ever trust themselves to love again. They are afraid of being hurt again.

Trust is a major part of love, and people who have been hurt don't want to be hurt anymore. To keep from being hurt again from the lack of love, these same people will put up different defense mechanisms to guard their hearts and feelings from being hurt. So many people today are afraid and fearful of loving. But fear is our enemy, for God's Word says that he did not give us a spirit of fear but that he gave us "love, power and a sound mind" (2 Timothy 1:7 AMP).

Also 1 John 4:18 tells us that "perfect love cast out the spirit of fear." Some people who are afraid to love want to love more than anything, but they are in a prison from a past experience of being hurt, so they refuse to walk in love or allow themselves to be loved. These people see no way of ever getting out from the prison of no love.

Dear friend, there is a way out, and it is through the precious blood of Jesus Christ. Jesus is the way, the truth, and the light. The light of God's love will shine through the darkness in your soul and guide you toward true love—God love. God's love came to set the captives free. As the Word says, whomever Jesus set free is free indeed. You may ask yourself, "How can I get out of this prison of no love?" Well, just call on the name of the Lord Jesus right where you are. Ask him for help, and be truthful with him, and be truthful with yourself. Tell him that you want out, and you want to love again or to experience true love for the very first time. Tell him that you need to experience love and give love but that you don't know how or where to begin. As you open yourself to love, you must understand that pain and hurt may come again, but allow yourself to be loved and give love as if no one has or will ever hurt you. Allow God's love to flow in and through your life. Be a vessel of his love.

We must learn to overlook people's offenses because if we don't, we will walk around in the bondage and pain of people hurting us. Most of us have heard the saying that "hurting people hurt people." Some people have the mentality that, "I'm going to hurt them before they hurt me." Every day, practice overlooking the pain that someone is or may be trying to cause you. Don't allow the spirits of frustration and aggravation interfere with your love walk. There are spirits that will try to stop you from operating in the love of God. Walk in love, regardless, and learn to forgive; this will keep you free from the spirit of offense. In other words, learn to forgive as much as possible.

Remember that the Word of God tells us "to guard our hearts because out of it flows the issues of life" (Proverbs 4:23). We should not harbor ill feelings in our hearts and minds. Remember that in the spiritual realm, our minds and hearts are one and the same. As a man (woman] thinks in his (her) heart, so is he (she) (Proverbs 23:7 AMP).

There is a famous quote from Marcus Aurelius, an emperor of Ancient Rome: "A man's life is what his thoughts make of it." Therefore, we should keep our hearts clear and pure because this is what God loves and looks for. Ask God the Father to create in you a clean heart and to renew a right spirit within you, just like King David did in Psalm 51:10. God honored and blessed King David because he was honest and truthful with where his heart was.

Once you are out of the prison of no love, you must make sound decisions and be determined that you never will go back behind those bars of imprisonment again. Fight for your freedom to love and be loved because it is a daily battle. Every day of your life, you will be faced with the choice of either holding on to pain and hurt from your past and present or walking in love. Sometimes, others will bring you their pain and hurt, just to cause you pain and hurt, but reject it and show the depth of God's love, even to those who mean you no good. The power of God's love can conquer all things, but we must have faith in it. The Bible tells us that it is impossible to please God without faith. Well, faith in what? We must have faith in the power of God's love, which is real. If we do not exercise faith in the power of God's love, it cannot and will not work for us. We need love for our faith to work anyway, and we need faith for our love to work. And without faith, it is impossible to please God.

> But without faith it is impossible to [walk with God and] please Him, for whoever comes [near] to God must [necessarily] believe that God exists and that He rewards those who [earnestly and diligently] seek Him. (Hebrews 11:6 AMP)

Without love and faith together, neither will work,

> For [if we are] in Christ Jesus neither circumcision nor un-circumcision means anything, but only faith activated and expressed and working through love. (Galatians 5:6 AMP)

Love and faith—both are needed together in order to work.

For us to be committed to anything, we need faith and love, especially when we are faced with daily life issues. Each day, we must make a choice to do something with our pain and hurt. What are you going to do with yours? Are you going to exercise your faith and release pain and hurt to God, or are you going to hold on to it? Will you begin each day with a commitment to walk in God's love, or will you go back to the prison of no love? Friend, you've got to fight the good fight of faith and stay free to walk in God's love. We walk in God's love by daily communicating with him through: prayer, reading, and meditating on God's Word. Spend some time with him so that you can be empowered to walk in God's love. This is the only way to stay free to love God's way.

To walk in God's love is to walk in the supernatural. And we walk in the supernatural, again, through prayer, reading, and meditating on his Word. If you try to love in your ability, you will fail to love, but remember that God's love is a powerful force that will never fail. His love is his Spirit and his presence that is alive and active, which helps and empowers us to love when love seems impossible, especially when in a difficult place.

We can walk in God's love and move by his power in several ways:

Be aware of your inner person, your spiritual person. Be aware and make a daily assessment of where you are spiritually, and be truthful with yourself. If something is not right in your spirit, go to God in prayer and repent, and he will help you to get yourself together.

Be committed to daily devotions through prayer, reading, and studying the Word of God. We should commune with God the Father on a daily basis. Meditate on his love for you and his promises. Listen to the Word, and speak and confess the Word over yourself.

Submit and surrender to God the Father all ill feelings you may be harboring. Cleanse your heart daily. Psalm 51:10 reminds you to ask God to create in you a clean heart and renew a right spirit within you. This was King David's prayer to God.

In order for God to pour his love in your heart, your heart must be cleansed and surrendered to him. Keep dumping your heart out to God daily. God's love cannot come into a heart that wants to hold on to or is filled with ill feelings and evilness. Make sure you desire to have heart that is pleasing to God. And if it's not pleasing to God, ask him to come into your heart and clean it out because you want a pure heart that pleases God. God the Father is looking for those who want a pure heart that is pleasing to him. Believe it or not, apart from God, we can do nothing, not even processing a pure heart for him that glorifies him in every way.

Walk in forgiveness and practice being kind to other people. Learn to smile and learn to laugh again.

> Lift up your heads, O gates,
> And be lifted up, ancient doors,
> That the King of glory may come in.
> Who is the King of glory?
> The Lord strong and mighty,
> The Lord mighty in battle.
> Lift up your heads, O gates,
> And lift them up, ancient doors,

That the King of glory may come in

Psalm 24:7-9

> So lift up your head and live again. There is always something to live for. The Word of God also says, "Anyone who is among the living has hope—even a live dog is better off than a dead lion!" (Ecclesiastes 9:4).

Daily cast your cares and anxieties on God the Father. Cast all your cares on him because he cares for you,

> Casting all your cares [all your anxieties, all your worries, and all your concerns, once and for all] on Him, for He cares about you [with deepest affection, and watches over you very carefully]. (1 Peter 5:7 AMP)

We must never forget to also be thankful and joyful and to remember to pray about everything.

> Rejoice always and delight in your faith; be unceasing and persistent in prayer; in every situation [no matter what the circumstances] be thankful and continually give thanks to God; for this is the will of God for you in Christ Jesus. (1 Thessalonians 5:16–18 AMP)

Learn to trust God to help you to love the unlovable. Remember to ask him to help you and walk in his love.

Practice, practice, practice walking in love because practice makes perfect. Practice brings about maturity in a thing. The more you practice your love walk, the more you become mature in love. Never give up. Always keep trying to walk in love.

Remember that love never fails, and understand that if you give love and sow love, love will find its way back to you. You always reap what you have sown.

Six

Show Me Your Love

Deuteronomy 6:5
John 13:34–35; 15:9–10, 14; 21:15–17
1 John 2:3–6; 3:4–10; 14:21
Psalm 122:1
Matthew 10:42; 22:37–38; 25:35–40
Mark 12:28–34
Hebrews 6:10
1 Corinthians13
Galatians 5:13–14

You shall love the Lord your God with all your heart and mind and with all your soul and with all your strength [your entire being]. (Deuteronomy 6:5 AMP)

And Jesus replied to him, "You shall love the Lord your God with all your heart, and with all your soul, and with all your mind." This is the first and greatest commandment. (Matthew 22:37–38 AMP)

Too often, we tell God that we love him and how much we really care for him. There will be times in our lives, however, when God will confront us with the spirit of truth, the inner witness, and ask us to prove our love for him. "Prove it," the Spirit of the Lord will say, like any lover will say from time to time, requesting proof or a demonstration of love. Lately, have you demonstrated your love for God; and if so, how? Is there any proof in your daily life that you love the Lord? Bless God if you have acknowledged your love and honor for God, but I pray for those of us who have not come to understand the importance of expressing our love for God. Sad to say, but some of us will continue to ignore God's request to show love from us.

Remember that love is a spiritual force that comes through a decision and action. If you love someone, you will show it. To say you love someone but never show it is no validation of your love for him or her.

The Word of God lets us know and understand that God desires for us to demonstrate our love for him. Ephesians 5:10 says, "Find out what pleases the Lord." We get caught up in trying to please everyone else around us, rather than the one who created us. In order for us to show God that we love him, we must find out what pleases him. Just as we find out what pleases the people in our lives whom we love, we must do the same for God the Father. What makes them smile? What makes them happy or sad? What displeases them? Well, friend, God wants that same type of attention and affection from us. We need to find out from God what we do to make him happy and joyful and what we do to displease him. If we are in tune with our inner man, the Holy Spirit, he will always let us know what pleases God (1

Corinthians 2:6–16). The inner witness, the spirit of God on the inside of us, tells us what he likes and dislikes. As a matter of fact, if we were to study the Word of God, we would find out most of what pleases God.

Take, for instance, Proverbs 6:16—there are six things that God says he hates and seven things that are an abomination to him. Most of us don't know what they are, nor have we tried to find out. The Word of God is loaded with things that God dislikes and likes, but we don't spend any time trying to find out. First Thessalonians tell us to be joyful, pray always, and thank God in everything in Christ Jesus because this is God's will for everyone. Unless we spend time with God and his Word, we will not know his will for us. How can we claim to love him if we are not seeking to please him?

Prove It—Where Is Your Love

And Jesus replied to him, "'YOU SHALL LOVE THE LORD YOUR GOD WITH ALL YOUR HEART, AND WITH ALL YOUR SOUL, AND WITH ALL YOUR MIND.' This is the first and greatest commandment. The second is like it, 'YOU SHALL LOVE YOUR NEIGHBOR AS YOURSELF [that is, unselfishly seek the best or higher good for others].' The whole Law and the [writings of the] Prophets depend on these two commandments."

Matthew 22:37–40

According to these two texts, Christians failed to love God the Father with all of their hearts, souls, and strength. I believe the text is really saying that we should love the Lord God with our spirit-men, which represent our hearts and our minds, by meditating and thinking on his Word, his goodness, and his loving kindness. Love God with all our souls, which is our action, our will, our emotion, and our intelligence. Loving God with our strength represents our talents and our gifts with which he has blessed us. Basically, we need to love God with everything we have within us, in the spiritual realm as well as in the natural realm. If we love God in the spiritual realm, it will cause the natural realm, our natural man, to submit to a loving God. When we totally love God with everything we have, I believe we will not go wrong. He wants to have top priority in our lives. If we put God first in every area of our lives, we will live victoriously and succeed in life because we will understand how and why we were created.

So many, of us go wrong because we neglect to demonstrate our love for God the Father, others, and ourselves. We allow so many things to replace our affection for and attention to God. God tells us that he is a jealous God in Exodus 20:5. Yes, jealousy is evil and wrong. How can a good God become jealous? God has every right to become jealous over us because he created and knows us, and he wants what is best for us. He loves us more than we could possibly love ourselves. God's jealousy is justified through his love for and over us. When we are jealous, it is not justified; we cannot justify our jealous feelings in any shape or form. The type of jealousy that God has is not the same as the jealousy we experience. People who operate in any form of jealousy have evil intentions and motives behind their feelings of jealousy; they don't want what is best for the person of whom they are jealous of. But not God; it is his desire that we have the best possible life we can have, with him at the center of it. In John 10:10, Jesus told us that "he came that we may have life and have it more abundantly."

We should have no other God before the one and only true and living God. We are so quick to make gods out of other people, such as spouses, children, bosses, and friends. We make gods out of our careers (even ministries), hobbies, and our quest for learning (education). Sometimes, we even make gods out of things, like houses, cars, money, and clothing.

In Matthew 10:37, Jesus says, "Anyone who loves his father or mother more than me is not worthy of me; anyone who loves his son or daughter more than me is not worthy of me." None of those things and no one can ever give us what God can give us every time--the enjoyment of having things that last momentarily; then we are off, seeking enjoyment and pleasure in something new. Most times, we humans are rarely satisfied and never content with what we have. There is nothing wrong with having and enjoying nice and beautiful things, but to replace them with our love for the heavenly Father is backwards. God said that he gave us all things to richly enjoy but not to replace him (1 Timothy 6:17).

Religious people don't have the love of God; they have a form of godliness, but they have denied the power (love) of Christ within their very souls. Some believe that we are living in the last days, when people love money, themselves, and the pleasure thereof, rather than loving God (2 Timothy 3:1–5). Even among the brothers and sisters of Christ, we find that people don't really have the God kind of love for one another the way they should. And so the question now becomes; are you a saint or are you just religious? Because the saints of God possess the love of God; they walk in it, regardless of the situation or circumstance around them. The Word of God says that one example of the evidence of being a Christian is someone who possesses the God kind of love. People and things are not supposed to replace our love, attention, and affection for God. It hurts God and grieves him when we put people and things before him.

Sometimes, we lose our way and forget how much God really loves us. God desires to be intimate with us. He is the lover of our souls (Psalm 42:1). Just as the deer pants after the water of the brook, God wants our souls to thirst for more of him. And as we thirst for more of him, we, in turn, desire to give God more of ourselves. He desires that we demonstrate our love towards him. God wants an intimate kind of love, where two become one. God desires a love relationship with us in which he will come in and abide with us and be one with us, just as he and Jesus were one and just as husbands and wives become one when they marry (John 17:20–21).

Sharing the Gospel

One of the most important ways in which we show our love for God is by sharing the gospel with others and by caring for others. John 21:15–17 tells us of the last time that Jesus appeared to the disciples. After he finished dining with them on the beach, he turned to Simon Peter, the one who claimed to have loved him, and questioned Peter's love for him—just as we would do, perhaps after a nice dinner or beautiful time with a lover; we would ask, "Do you love me?"

"Yes, I love you, Jesus," Peter answered a second time.

Jesus looked Peter straight in the eyes and asked, "Do you love me, Peter?"

"Of course I love you, Jesus; you know that I do."

"Then take care of my sheep."

Jesus wants us to be kind and affectionate to each other by showing brotherly love toward one another. That is how we demonstrate our love for God the Father.

A third time, Jesus looked at Peter very seriously and asked, "Do you love me?"

Peter was now offended because Jesus has repeatedly asked him in front of the other disciples if he loved him, and Peter felt as if he was on the spot.

Jesus finally said again, "Then feed my sheep." In other words, tell people about me and evangelize about me.

When we love someone, we will tell everybody we meet about him or her. Just for one minute, think of your first love and how you told everybody about that person. We told our friends at school and the people at work. Some of us were so in love that we even told our enemies or people we did not know personally about those we loved. Who have you told about Jesus lately?

Caring for Others

In Matthew 25:35–40, Jesus describes that we demonstrate our love for God the Father by caring for others. If we possess God's love, we will care for others.

This text is plain and simple on how we are to minister the love of God. The Word says,

> For I was hungry and you gave me food; I was thirsty and you gave me drink; I was a stranger and you took me in ; I was naked and you clothed me; I was sick and you visited me; I was in prison and you came to me. Then the righteous will answer him, saying, Lord, "when did we see you hungry and feed you or thirsty and give you drink? When did we see you as a stranger and take you in, or naked and clothe you? Or when did we see you sick or in prison and come to see you? And the King will answer and say to them, "Assuredly, I say to you, in as much as you did it to one of the least of these my brethren, you did it to me." (Matthew 25:35–40)

Too often, we, as Christians, talk a lot about how much we love the Lord, but we don't express it in any way. We want to serve him, but when it comes time to demonstrate our love for God and to care for those less fortunate than us, we miss the mark. Now, we cannot care for the needs of everyone around us, but we can help some of them some of the time. Jesus did say we would always have the poor with us. Needy people and those less fortunate than us will always exist, but again, we can make a difference with the power of God's love for the betterment of someone else's life.

Believe it or not, there are people who do not know

or can't comprehend the extent of God's love for them. Hebrews 6:10 says that God "will not forget the love you have shown his people." Stop showing favoritism toward those who have positions, titles, and possessions. Don't do things for just those who can do something for you because that's not true love. Minister the love of God to everyone around you, especially those who are less fortunate, who may not know God or be able to do anything. Make an effort to introduce God to those who may not have had the chance to get to know of him, especially his love. Let God love them through you. Everybody is somebody in the eyes of God because we are all his creation. For everything that God made, he said it was good. One day, we will be held accountable for how we cared for others and demonstrated God's love toward them.

Critical Love

The Word of God also tells us of a critical view of demonstrating our love for God by keeping his commandments. "If you love me keep my commandments" (John 14:15). This is one of the major areas that we all neglect or struggle with in demonstrating our love for God.

> If ye keep my commandments ye shall abide in my love; even as I kept my Father's commandments, and abide in his love. (John 15:10)

Holy living is a high form of demonstrating our love for God. Desiring and trying to live to please God is our service

Seven

What Does Love Have to Do with It?

John 15:9–17
1 Corinthians 13:18

The Excellence of Love

> If I speak with the tongues of men and of
> angels, but have not love [for others growing
> out of God's love for me], then I have become
> only a noisy gong or a clanging cymbal [just
> an annoying distraction]. And if I have the
> gift of prophecy [and speak a new message
> from God to the people], and understand
> all mysteries, and [possess] all knowledge;
> and if I have all [sufficient] faith so that I
> can remove mountains, but do not have love
> [reaching out to others], I am nothing. If I
> give all my possessions to feed the poor, and
> if I surrender my body to be burned, but

do not have love, it does me no good at all. Love endures with patience and serenity, love is kind and thoughtful, and is not jealous or envious; love does not brag and is not proud or arrogant. It is not rude; it is not self-seeking, it is not provoked [nor overly sensitive and easily angered]; it does not take into account a wrong endured. It does not rejoice at injustice, but rejoices with the truth [when right and truth prevail]. Love bears all things [regardless of what comes], believes all things [looking for the best in each one], hopes all things [remaining steadfast during difficult times], and endures all things [without weakening], Love never fails [it never fades nor ends]. But as for prophecies, they will pass away; as for tongues, they will cease; as for the gift of special knowledge, it will pass away. (1 Corinthians 13:1–8 AMP)

I have loved you just as the Father has loved Me; remain in My love [and do not doubt My love for you]. If you keep My commandments and obey My teaching, you will remain in My love, just as I have kept My Father's commandments and remain in His love. I have told you these things so that My joy and delight may be in you, and that your joy may be made full and complete and overflowing. (John 15:9–17 AMP)

Not long ago, there was a popular rock and roll song by Tina Turner titled "What's Love Got to Do with It." Most of us were clear that this song was written as a result of the abuse Tina suffered from her ex-husband, Ike Turner. She suffered emotional, verbal, mental, and extreme physical abuse. On several occasions, he almost killed her. Tina, however, was able to survive and move on with her life. I'm also very clear that it was God's grace, mercy, and love that brought Tina through the ordeal with her ex-husband. She had to reach deep down inside herself and tap into God's love in order to not only survive but live to continue to bless us with her calling—her talent, her great music, her purpose in life through the years.

In John 15:16, God reminds us that we did not choose him, but he has chosen us. In the same breath, he reminds us of the commandment to love each other. Why, in the midst of his calling and choosing us for a particular reason, would he remind us to love one another? I believe he is reminding us of his love that he has placed in us so that we have the power to do what he created us for. If we are going to live the life that God the Father has planned for us, and if we are going to bear good fruit that will last, then we must possess the spirit of love.

Why the spirit of love, you may ask, and not other gifts of the Spirit—like courage, for instance? Simple: because the spirit of love is the evidence of God's presence, manifested in us. When we walk in God's love, not only are we walking in his presence but we are walking in his power, and we will produce evidence of good fruit, like courage, fearlessness, patience, and kindness. In John 4:7–8, the Word clearly states that God is love. Now remember, love is not weak, but love is all-powerful, and it will never fail. Why does something like love never fail? Because love is God, and God is love, and God never fails (1 Corinthians 13:8).

This is why some people can operate in love toward people who have deeply hurt them—because of God's love operating in them. God's love is; his power; or let's just say God's empowerment. I disagree with Sister Tina's song— that love is a "second-hand emotion." She sang out of her pain with a catchy tune and the abuse she went through, but I understand why she sang that song the way she did. Her healing process was not finished, or perhaps she was reflecting on the pain she once experienced. Sometimes, it's very hard to love when one relives pain and hurt from the past, rehashing it over and over again—the thing that brought trauma. When people operate out of pain and hurt, I believe it is a signal that they are not fully healed, and they are still hurting. Healing is a process, and for some people, it will take a lifetime to be healed. The timing of healing is not same for everyone, but I believe that if we allow God's love to flow through us and in us, our healing processes will be a lot quicker, complete, and lacking nothing.

A lot of us have been abused, mistreated, hurt, and sometimes left for dead, but through God's grace, we survived to love again. I've mentioned the idea that hurting people will hurt people, and I've learned that this is true. Through God's grace, however, we can and will survive hurt and pain. If we hold on to hope, the power of God's love will come to rescue us. Some of us have been rescued or are being rescued from the dead—not a physical death but perhaps an emotional and/or spiritual death.

There is so much in the world that is designed to kill

people, spiritually, emotionally, and mentally, but if we allow God's love to come in and empower us, it will revive us to live and love again. Love is an anointing, an empowerment, and a spiritual force from God that helps and empowers us to do whatever we need to do. Again, God is love, and love is God. The spirit of love is God's presence. God's love empowers us to do supernatural things that we can't explain or can't do in our own strength. His love can empower us to forgive when forgiveness is impossible. This kind of empowerment will step in and rescue us from our darkest days of pain and hurt and show us a way out when there seems to be none.

Our heavenly Father will create a way out for your deliverance, if need be, when there is no way out. Throughout the Bible, we see the power of love working through the lives of people from all walks of life. There is power in God's love, but unfortunately, most of us do not seek it or operate in it because we do not believe in the power of his love and that it will never fail us. Unfortunately, most times we try to figure out things in our own strength, and that is where we fall short of empowerment to live a life filled with God's love.

Too often, we do not allow the spirit of love, the empowerment of God, to come in, minister to us, and work through us. Day in and day out, we go through life, struggling, trying to make it on our own strength instead of operating in his love. Some of us don't realize that we are carrying pain, resentment, bitterness, and hatred in us, rather than abiding in God and letting his love, Spirit, and power abide in and through our lives. Sometimes, abiding in God is a matter of simply calling and crying out to him in truth.

After crying out to God, the Spirit of truth will come and speak to your heart. The Holy Spirit will always commune with you and reveal to you something you need to know. Stop avoiding the Spirit of truth, and deal with what he is trying to say to you. When the Spirit of truth comes, don't ignore him or deny the truth he is speaking because it is from God—actually, it is God.

Have you ever heard someone say, "Someone told me ..." this or that? That inner voice speaks on behalf of God, Holy Spirit, and the Spirit of truth. The Holy Spirit that speaks for God is part of the Godhead—one God in three persons—and the Holy Spirit is the third person of the Godhead, the holy Trinity. The union of three persons in one is the holy Trinity—Father, Son and the Holy Ghost/Spirit.

God is listening, so tell him how people have mistreated you. Tell him where the pain is. Tell him what they did to you. And tell him your hopes and dreams. Trust and believe that you can tell him how you really feel, and then ask him to help you. Then wait and let him help you. Stop asking God for help but then go back to your old way of doing things and not allow him to help you. When the struggles of life come, don't get bitter, nasty, critical, and mean. Walk in God's love because it is available to you. Love will keep you when you cannot be kept. Love will bless you right where you need to be blessed.

God's love will strengthen you where you need to be strengthened. The power of Love can open doors that no one can shut. God's love is our divine helper and healer; that is why Jesus reminds us of how much he loves us and to remain in his love. Jesus also tells us throughout the scriptures that if we will acknowledge God the Father and his power, God's unfailing love is available to empower and help us. We must remember that if we don't have love, the Word says we have nothing. Apart from God, we have and can do nothing.

> I am the Vine; you are the branches. The one who remains in Me; and I in him bears much fruit, for [otherwise] apart from Me [that is, cut off from vital union with Me] you can do nothing. (John 15:5 AMP)

God does not care how anointed or spiritually gifted you are. We need love. Money, status, positions, and fame are all well and good, but in order to live the abundant life that Jesus talks about in John 10:10, we need the spirit of love. Believe it or not, love is one of the highest forms of spiritual warfare. This is why Jesus tells us to love our enemies. Love is one of the spiritual gifts that God has given to everyone. In the midst of trouble and chaos, most of us panic and forget the power of love, God, and Jesus. Our lives would have less hurt, pain, and turmoil if we would acknowledge and walk in love more often. But to walk in love will take effort on our part.

I'm not saying that it is easy, but you can do it, with the help of the Father. Reflect on those times when you allowed God's love to operate through you. Think of a time when you came out of trouble much quicker when you walked in love. If you just took a moment to realize how God's love rescued you, maybe when it was about to turn for the worst, you would operate in love more often. Practice makes perfect, so practice your love walk today, right where you are. The more you practice walking in love, the better you will become at it.

Friend, if you want power for living, then check your love walk. Our love walk has a lot to do with everything that concerns us. If we experience a lot of confusion, trouble, and failure, we must look at our love walks because when all else fails, love will never fail. Love never fails, but we fail to love. We fail to operate in that which God commands us to operate from the beginning. How is your love walk?

One of the most powerful men who ever lived on the face of this earth was Jesus, God in the flesh. And Jesus had a serious love walk. To walk in love may not be easy, but it is worth it. It may be hard at first, but it can become easier the more you learn and practice walking in it. Learn to walk in love one step at a time—one day, one moment, and one experience at a time—and love will not fail you. Remember, God first calls us to love one another. So be very clear when the abuse comes and an unpleasant situation finds your address. Ask yourself this one question: what does love have to do with it? And the answer, my friend, is *everything*. Peace and love.

Eight

Prayer and Instruction for a Redeemed Life

Staying Focused and Flexible

Worshipping God through the power of love and prayer will always shift the atmosphere and our mindsets for the good. When we need to know and understand and need help with our love walk, we can cry out to God in midst of the valley of dry bones—no love. As we call out to God to walk in love, we can be reassured that he will answer, and our valley of dry bones will come alive. The enemy has to shut his mouth as we live again, worshipping God through our love walk. We glorify God by trusting him and choosing to walk in love even when it is difficult. Trusting God and deciding to continuously walk in love will cause us to live in victory in every season of life. When the enemy of our souls comes up against us to hinder or dismiss our dreams, talents, gifts, and opportunities, our worshipping through love will stop the enemy in his tracks against us.

Our love walk will always be our road to break through, breaking the back of the enemy. Problems, trouble, and trials may come to destroy us, but our love walk will be a witness to abundant victory and a greater level of living. Please know that if we do not faint in our season of testing and trials and choose to walk in love, we will reap blessings, due to a shift in the atmosphere because of our focus, flexibility, and choice to walk and live in God's love.

Dear friend, in order to possess the kingdom of God here on earth and be in covenant with God the Father, we first must know and understand who our heavenly Father is, and that's through a personal relationship with his Son, Jesus Christ. The only way we can have this relationship is by accepting Jesus Christ as our personal Lord and Savior. We can do this by first believing that Jesus Christ is Lord, confessing our sins, and purposely turning from a lifestyle of sin, death, destruction, and damnation. We can surrender our lives to God by praying this simple prayer and allowing him to fill our hearts with his Holy Spirit:

Father, in the name of Jesus, I recognize and acknowledge that I am a sinner. I now repent and purposefully turn from a life of sin, death, and destruction. I confess with my mouth and believe in my heart that Jesus Christ is Lord and that you raised him from the dead. I invite you, Lord Jesus, to come into my heart, into my life, and fill me with your Holy Spirit. Guide and lead with your love. Thank you, Lord, for saving me. Amen.

> Because if you acknowledge and confess with your mouth that Jesus is Lord [recognizing His power, authority, and

majesty as God], and believe in your heart that God raised Him from the dead, you will be saved. For with the heart a person believes [in Christ as Savior] resulting in his justification [that is, being made righteous—being freed of the guilt of sin and made acceptable to God]; and with the mouth he acknowledges and confesses [his faith openly], resulting in and confirming [his] salvation. (Roman 10:9–10 AMP)

Welcome to the family of God. Ephesians 2:19 tells us that we are "no longer foreigners and aliens, but fellow citizens with God's people and members of God's household." Now that you have prayed and confessed Jesus as your Lord and Savior, I pray that you will follow the simple instruction to develop a strong spiritual walk (life).

Pray, study, and obey God's Word daily. Be joyful and purposely walk in love (2 Timothy 3:16; 1 Thessalonians 5:16–18).

Find and join a good Bible-believing church. Be faithful and committed in a local church. Don't let anything or anyone turn you back (Hebrews 10:25).

Get baptized by water (Matthew 3:6).

Pray and ask the Holy Spirit to baptize in the Spirit with the evidence of speaking in tongues (Acts 2:3–4).

Remember that God's love will never fail you (John 3:16; 2 Corinthians 13:8).

If you fall in your daily walk with God, remember his love, get back up, and repent by purposefully turning away from sin, and keep on walking with God.

Love Prayer

Put on love daily by praying and purposefully walking in it. Hallelujah to the Lord God Almighty.

Father, in the name of Jesus, I bless your holy name, and I thank you for your love. Today, may I abide in and walk in your perfect love, toward you, others, and myself. Where I'm weak, strengthen me with your love, and where I'm strong, help me to share your love. Amen.

> So, as God's own chosen people, who are holy [set apart, sanctified for His purpose] and well-beloved [by God Himself], put on a heart of compassion, kindness, humility, gentleness, and patience [which has the power to endure whatever injustice or unpleasantness comes, with good temper]; bearing graciously with one another, and willingly forgiving each other if one has a cause for complaint against another; just as the Lord has forgiven you, so should you forgive. Beyond all these things put on and wrap yourselves in [unselfish] love, which is the perfect bond of unity [for everything is bound together in agreement when each one seeks the best for others]. (Colossians 3:12–14 AMP)

Scripture References to Become Familiar With

2 Corinthians 4:8; 5:17–18; 10:5, 13
John 5:38–40; 14:1, 23–24
Mark 24:4
Romans 8:2
Hebrews 12:1–2; 13:5–6
Judges 10:13
James 1:2–18; 2:1, 22–25
Luke 4:8
Psalm 34:19; 42:5; 51:10; 55:22, 91; 138:8
Colossians 1:13, 27
Proverbs 5:18; 10:24
Philippians 4:4–8
Job 23:1
Jeremiah 29:11

Bibliography

Augustusel, Vernadette R. *Being Committed in a Difficult Place.* Bloomington, IN: WestBow Press, 2020.

Augustusel, Vernadette R. *Don't Worry, Worship; Worship, Don't Worry.* Bloomington, IN: WestBow Press, 2017.

Benokraitis, Nijole V. *Marriages and Families: Changes, Changes, Choices and Constraints.* Upper Saddle River, NJ: Prentice Hall,1996

Bowden, John. *The Westminster Dictionary of Christian Theology.* Edited by Alan Richardson. Philadelphia: The Westminster Press, 1983.

The New Testament Greek Lexicon. www.studylight.org.

The Old Testament Hebrew Lexicon. www.studylight.org.

Printed in the United States
by Baker & Taylor Publisher Services